Genre Biography

? **Essential Question**
What do heroes do?

Rudy Garcia-Tolson
by Ann Weil

Chapter 1

A Hero Who Has No Legs

Before Rudy Garcia-Tolson became a Paralympic swimmer, he faced many challenges at birth.

Rudy was born with **physical** challenges. These challenges affected the way his body looked and worked. There were problems with his mouth and hands. There were serious problems with his legs. Rudy had a hard time walking. Everyday tasks were difficult for Rudy. But he didn't let challenges stop him from going after his dreams.

Jason Dewey Photography

Young Rudy showed courage. He hoped to walk and play like other children. But because of problems with his legs, he needed surgery. Doctors tried to fix the problems. Rudy had many **operations**, but doctors couldn't fix everything. Rudy thought he might need a wheelchair for the rest of his life.

Doctors said they could give him new legs. First, they would need to remove Rudy's old legs. Rudy and his family decided he would have the operation.

Doctors help people decide what to do.

When Rudy was five years old, doctors removed his legs. Then he got artificial, or man-made, legs. The new legs were very strong. They were made of metal and plastic. Rudy could now stand and move easily. These legs changed Rudy's life!

Arms and legs like this one help people without hands or legs to walk and hold things.

4

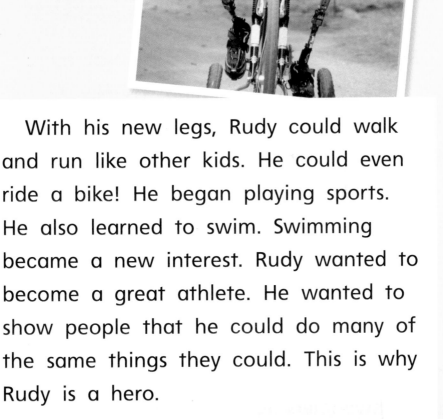

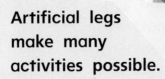

Artificial legs make many activities possible.

With his new legs, Rudy could walk and run like other kids. He could even ride a bike! He began playing sports. He also learned to swim. Swimming became a new interest. Rudy wanted to become a great athlete. He wanted to show people that he could do many of the same things they could. This is why Rudy is a hero.

Rudy can swim faster than most swimmers with two legs.

Rudy loved to swim. He did not need his new legs for swimming. Usually, swimmers kick their legs to move faster. Rudy did not kick his legs. He began to discover that he could use his strong upper body and arms. He could swim quickly through the water. Rudy practiced every day. He got better and better.

Rudy entered swimming races. He won first place in many races. It was hard for other swimmers to catch him in the pool!

Rudy competed in other events. He tried **triathlons**. In a triathlon, people usually swim, bike, and run. Most athletes need to change their shoes for the running and biking parts of the race. Rudy changes his legs! He uses longer legs for biking. He uses shorter legs for running. When Rudy was 10 years old, he became the youngest person without legs to finish a triathlon on his own.

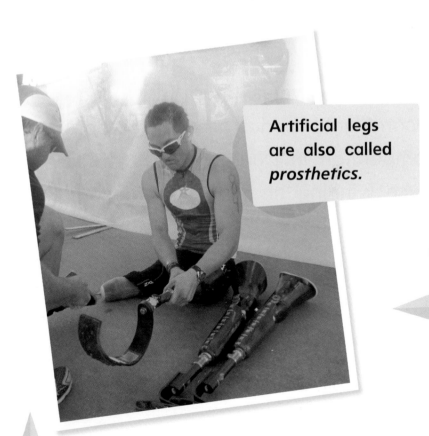

Artificial legs are also called *prosthetics.*

Rudy has competed in the Paralympic Games. When Rudy was 16, he won his first gold medal at the Games in Athens, Greece. Two years later, he won a second gold medal at a major paralympic competition in Durban, South Africa. Since winning his first gold medals, Rudy has set swimming records.

The Paralympic Games are like the Olympic Games. Athletes compete for medals. Both competitions are held the same year and at the same place. The difference is that Paralympic athletes have a disability.

chapter 3

An Athlete's Life

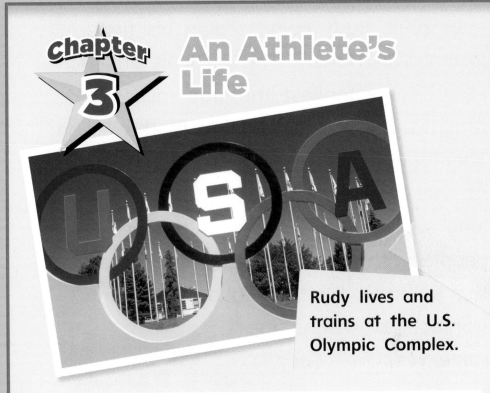

Rudy lives and trains at the U.S. Olympic Complex.

Andre Jenny/Alamy

Rudy lives in Colorado at a **training center**. He works out during the day. Rudy also meets with doctors who study artificial legs and feet. They want to help improve Rudy's legs. With their help, Rudy can perform better. Living at the training center helps Rudy improve his skills. He hangs out with other athletes and eats healthful food. Rudy takes care of himself so he can succeed.

In 2009, Rudy competed in his first Ironman in Hawaii. This difficult athletic event is the longest triathlon race. Athletes begin by swimming in the ocean. Then they bike through the mountains. At the end of the race, they run a very long way. Rudy was one of the first people without both legs to compete in the Ironman. He finished a challenging Ironman in Arizona the same year.

Rudy puts on his legs for the biking part of the race.

In the Ironman race, athletes first swim 2.4 miles (3.86 km). Next, they bike 112 miles (180.25 km). Then they run 26.2 miles (42.2 km). Everyone who finishes within the time allowed is called an Ironman.

Chapter 4

A True Hero

Rudy is a hero to many kids.

Ariel Skelley/CORBIS

A hero is someone who helps others. Some heroes save people from danger. People agree that Rudy is a different kind of hero. He is a good **role model**. He inspires people to achieve their dreams.

Rudy Garcia-Tolson

The Life of a Hero

1988 Rudy was born on September 14 in California.

1999 At age 10, Rudy became the youngest double above-the-knee amputee to compete in a triathlon on his own.

1985 •••• 1990 •••• 1995 •••• 2000 ••••

1993 At age 5, Rudy had both of his legs removed.

2003 Rudy was in *Teen People* magazine's "20 Teens Who Will Change the World."

2004 Rudy won the gold medal and set the world record in swimming at the Paralympic Games in Greece.

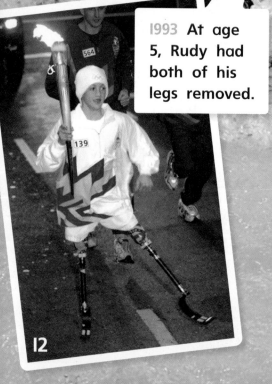

12

2016 Rudy competed in his fourth Paralympic Games in Brazil.

2005 •••• 2010 •••• 2015 •••• 2020

2007 Rudy moved to the Olympic Training Center.

2011 Rudy joined the Pan-Pacific Para-Swimming Championships U.S. team.

2008 Rudy won gold and bronze medals in swimming at the Paralympic Games in China.

Rudy shares his story with people around the country. He tells people about his life and encourages them to never give up. Rudy has a motto, or saying, that he lives by. His motto is, "A brave heart is a powerful weapon." This means that when you are not afraid, you can do anything. These are the words of a true hero.

Rudy often speaks in front of groups.

Respond to Reading

Summarize

Use important details to help you summarize *Rudy Garcia-Tolson.*

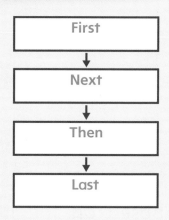

First

↓

Next

↓

Then

↓

Last

Text Evidence

1. How do you know that *Rudy Garcia-Tolson* is a biography? Genre

2. What happened in Rudy's childhood that led him to become an athlete? Sequence

3. Figure out the synonym for *challenging* on page 10. Synonyms

4. Write about what Rudy did in Greece in 2004. Write About Reading

Compare Texts
Read about another hero.

The Unsinkable Molly Brown

"Molly Brown" is both a hero and a legend. The legend of "Molly Brown" is based on the life of Margaret Brown. A legend mixes fact and fiction as it retells past events.

In 1912, Margaret Brown lived from 1867 to 1932. She was on a ship called the *Titanic*. When it sank, about 1,500 people died. Margaret Brown was one of about 700 people who survived.

Mrs. Brown's husband made a fortune from silver mines.

Everett Collection Inc/Alamy

Taking Charge

Picture this event. The *Titanic* was sinking fast. Margaret was pushed into a lifeboat. According to the legend, she did not rush to safety. Instead, she helped row the lifeboat to look for survivors.

Margaret's lifeboat was picked up by another ship. She was safe, but others were sick from the cold. She nursed these ill survivors. She also raised money for those who were poor.

The *Titanic* sank in 1912.

The Legend

Margaret was known as "Maggie" before she married. No one called her Molly. But when someone began writing a musical about her, he thought Molly sounded better. The result was a movie called *The Unsinkable Molly Brown.*

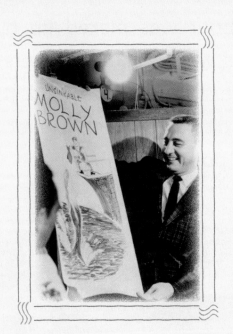

Musicals and movies about real people don't always stick to the facts.

Time & Life Pictures/Getty Images

Make Connections

What qualities make Margaret Brown a true hero? **Essential Question**

How are Rudy and Margaret similar?

Text to Text

Glossary

operations *(op-uh-RAY-shuhnz)* surgeries performed on a person's body to help that person get better *(page 3)*

physical *(FIZ-i-kuhl)* having to do with a person's body *(page 2)*

role model *(ROHL MOD-uhl)* a person other people try to be like *(page 11)*

training center *(TRAY-ning SEN-tur)* a place where athletes live and work out *(page 9)*

triathlons *(trigh-ATH-lonz)* three-part races, usually with swimming, biking, and running *(page 7)*

Index

Focus on
Social Studies

Purpose To identify a hero

What to Do

Step 1 ▶ Make a poster with the title "My Hero."

Step 2 ▶ Include your hero's name. List three things the person did that made him or her your hero.

Step 3 ▶ Draw a picture of each action.

Step 4 ▶ Share your poster with the class. Explain why you chose this hero.